A Lightworker's Guidebook

Prophecies for Humankind

as We Journey into the Age of Aquarius

Cindy Farries

A Lightworker's Guidebook: Prophecies for Humankind as we Journey into the Age of Aquarius © 2022 by Cindy Farries.

All rights reserved. No part of this book may be used or reproduced in any manner whatsoever, including internet usage, without written permission from the author, except in the case of a brief quotation under the terms of fair use.

Cover by Cindy Farries

ISBN: 978-1-7782807-0-2 (Paperback)

ISBN: 978-1-7782807-1-9 (E-book)

DEDICATION

I dedicate this book to Rhonda.

Without you, this book would not exist.

ACKNOWLEDGEMENTS

I would like to thank Rhonda from the bottom of my heart. Thank you for walking with me on this incredible journey and for helping to keep me grounded along the way. The process leading up to the writing of this book was a wild one, and I never would have made it through without you by my side. I am forever grateful for all the laughs and incredible moments and epiphanies along the way, and I'm so grateful that I have you to reminisce with and laugh all over again. I cannot thank you enough my beloved Soul Sister.

I would like to thank Colleen for being my life-long spiritual-journey friend. My spiritual journey started with you many, many years ago. I am forever grateful for all your support and kinship over the years. We have thousands of hours logged together, talking and exploring all kinds of spiritual topics as we learned and grew into ourselves. Nobody knows or understands me spiritually like you know me. Only you, Colleen. Only you.

CONTENTS

Introduction		1
Prophecy 1	Visitation	3
Prophecy 2	Miracles	4
Prophecy 3	Love will prevail	5
Prophecy 4	Portal of Love	6
Prophecy 5	Open Hearts	7
Prophecy 6	The Event	9
Prophecy 7	Life on Earth is special	10
Prophecy 8	Discovery in Stars	11
Prophecy 9	Miracles	12
Prophecy 10	Happiness and Joy	13
Prophecy 11	The Age of Aquarius	14
Prophecy 12	Lightworkers	15
Prophecy 13	Milestone events	16
Prophecy 14	New and exciting things	17
Prophecy 15	Unique place in the Universe	19
Prophecy 16	Free will experiment	20
Prophecy 17	Mass awakening	21
Prophecy 18	Euphoria	22
Prophecy 19	Unique talents	23
Prophecy 20	Earth in 100 years	25
Prophecy 21	Crystals	26
Prophecy 22	Love	27

Prophecy 23	Journey to Light	28
Prophecy 24	Premonitions	30
Prophecy 25	Health and Longevity	31
Prophecy 26	Weather and climate	32
Prophecy 27	End pain and suffering	34
Prophecy 28	Crystal magic wands	35
Prophecy 29	Ripple healing effect	36
Prophecy 30	Love energy effects	38
Prophecy 31	Council of the Universe	39
Prophecy 32	The divide	40
Prophecy 33	Blessings	41
Prophecy 34	Earth as over-seers	42
Prophecy 35	Changes	43
Prophecy 36	Free-will experiment	44
Prophecy 37	Stopping the descent	46
Prophecy 38	Joyful and creative	48
Prophecy 39	Lending Light	49
Prophecy 40	The Event	50
Prophecy 41	Power of Nature	51
Prophecy 42	The wind	52
Prophecy 43	Graduation	53
Prophecy 44	Hidden Treasures	54
Prophecy 45	Addiction	56
Prophecy 46	The Event	57
Prophecy 47	History of Earth	58

Prophecy 48	Love with be born	60
Prophecy 49	Karma	61
Prophecy 50	Living more	62
Prophecy 51	Open Hearts	63
Prophecy 52	Earth is challenging	64
Prophecy 53	Hope	66
Prophecy 54	Spreading Light	67
Prophecy 55	Life in 100 years	68
Prophecy 56	Soul Family	69
Prophecy 57	Job changes	70
Prophecy 58	Space Travel	71
Prophecy 59	Studying the Universe	72
Prophecy 60	Personal Work	73
Prophecy 61	Food	74
Prophecy 62	Animals	75
Prophecy 63	Reality	76
Prophecy 64	New Reality	77
Prophecy 65	Hope	78
Prophecy 66	Knowledge Library	79
Prophecy 67	Failure Karma	80
Prophecy 68	Connection	82
Prophecy 69	Children visit	83
Prophecy 70	New way to travel	85
Prophecy 71	The Event	86
Prophecy 72	Earth born in Love	87

Prophecy 73	The Event	88
Prophecy 74	Time	89
Prophecy 75	See through Time	90
Prophecy 76	Love effects	91
Prophecy 77	World Government	92
Prophecy 78	Tourists on Earth	93
Prophecy 79	Money	94
Prophecy 80	Angel guidance	95
Prophecy 81	Love is on her way	97
Prophecy 82	Big Karma	98
Prophecy 83	Chaos	99
Prophecy 84	Honour and Respect	100
Prophecy 85	Most satisfying	101
Prophecy 86	Treasured experience	102
Prophecy 87	Happy-go-lucky	103
Prophecy 88	Happiness	104
Prophecy 89	New Dimension	105
Prophecy 90	Lightworker dreams	106
Prophecy 91	New Dimension	107
Prophecy 92	Manifestation	108
Prophecy 93	Absent from Earth	109
Prophecy 94	A new way to travel	110
Prophecy 95	Balancing Power	111
Prophecy 96	Lightworker balance	112
Prophecy 97	Other galaxies	113

Prophecy 98	Love benefits All	114
Prophecy 99	Begin hoping	115
About the Author		117

Introduction

This book consists of channeled messages. The words in the prophecies are not mine. They are the words of one of my Guides who refers to herself as Victoria.

From the dates on the messages, it may seem like this book was written over the course of one month, but that was just the end of the process. The process leading up to the writing of this book started six and a half years ago. That's when I first learned how to use a pendulum and an alphabet mat to talk to my Angels and Guides.

When I first began to use my pendulum, I had to spell out each word, letter by letter. Within a month or two, I was able to know the word when the pendulum swung to the first letter. With practice, I've gotten faster and faster at channelling messages, with the help of my pendulum. I have been able to meet several of my Angels and Guides and I marvel at how their different personalities shine through in the way they talk and the energy I feel.

I love using my pendulum to help me channel messages because my Guides are really good at letting me know when I've gotten a word wrong. They do not hesitate to correct me and even get very specific with their corrections. They've stopped me mid-message to make sure I put an *s* on the end of *soul* to make it *souls*. They've corrected me when I've said *good* and they wanted me to say *great*. They get very specific about the words they say and how they word their messages.

Over the years, after countless hours of practice, I've learned to trust my Guides and how they word things. I trust them because I know that they will not hesitate to correct the smallest error if there is one. I also trust them because I've been working with them for years and the experience has been nothing short of magical and mind-blowing.

With that in mind, as I was writing this book, I made sure to write it exactly as I was given each message. I was corrected many times along the way and I asked for confirmation several times to ensure the wording and specific words used were correct. Every word in these prophecies is as Victoria intended it. Sometimes the wording makes more sense after the fact than it does before the message is realized. I've had a lot of experience with this phenomenon, and for that reason, I deliver the messages exactly as they were dictated to me.

I love the way Victoria has woven these prophecies together. She moves from one topic to another as she slowly builds a picture. Each time she comes back to a topic, she reveals a little more information so that it builds on top of itself as it goes around and around the topics, like a spiral. The spiral starts out low and slow and builds into a wonderful crescendo as it spirals upward, like a bloom bursting forth at the top of a spiraling vine growing towards the sun. I found the unfolding of all the messages simply fascinating, and I'm so grateful to have had this experience.

I hope you enjoy reading these messages as much as I've enjoyed receiving them. This has been a truly magical experience. I was surprised by some of the prophecies that came through and I am encouraged by the wonderful possibilities in our collective future. As with anything you would ever come across, I ask you to use your own discernment regarding these messages. Please take what resonates with you and leave the rest.

I wish you Peace, Joy and Happiness on your journey ahead.

Love and Light,

~Cindy~

June 30, 2022

Prophecy 1

Received May 31, 2022

Life on Earth is about to get very intense.

People will experience a wide range of emotions as never before felt on Earth.

People will become very afraid. Others will become very peaceful and calm.

There will be a visitation from beings who are not indigenous to Earth. This visitation will be witnessed around the world.

This visitation is a sign that Earth has passed a very significant test. This visitation is only possible when the energy on Earth is above the point of self-destruction.

This visitation is a cause for celebration. However, not everyone will see it as such. There will be many people who are going to be openly violent in the face of what they consider to be certain death.

Lightworkers will be called upon to hold the energy of peace and Love.

This chaotic period will only last a few months and will quickly morph Earth into a more unified and compassionate world.

Once the chaotic period ends, these visitors have a lot of knowledge to share with Earth.

This knowledge will not be shared with leaders of countries.

This knowledge will be shared with everyone.

This knowledge will change the power imbalance that has gripped Earth and its people for centuries.

This knowledge will bring power and peace to everyone.

Prophecy 2

Received June 1, 2022

Miracles are something that most people do not really believe in anymore.

Miracles were always part of Earth's experience. However, in the last century or so, miracles have been less and less common.

Lightworkers on Earth will begin to notice that miracles are becoming more commonplace once again.

The energy on Earth has passed a tipping point and Love is more dominant than fear.

Love has a lot to do with miracles on Earth.

Love energy has more power than most people realize.

Prophecy 3

Received June 2, 2022

Earth and its people are going to survive.

Earth and its people are going to thrive.

Earth and its people are going to hold a special place in the history of the Universe.

Earth and its people love more than any other beings.

Earth and its people have proven that free-will and Love can work together to create miracles.

Earth and its people have reincarnated over and over to prove that Love will prevail even when people are given free-will.

Earth and its people have given the Universe a huge gift of Love and knowledge. The beings of the Universe are forever indebted to Earth and its people for this unparalleled gift of Love and knowledge.

Earth and its people will reap the benefits of this gift.

Earth and its people are revered throughout the Universe.

Earth and its people are held in the highest honour and will be treated as dignitaries whenever they travel the Universe.

Prophecy 4

Received June 3, 2022

The world, and the Universe it is part of, are opening a portal of Love.

This portal of Love will change the lives of every person on Earth.

Miracles are going to become common, and people are going to create technology and manufacturing that will make it possible for every person on Earth to eat well and live well and play well.

Prophecy 5

Received June 4, 2022

The opening of a portal on Earth has occurred.

This portal allows Love energy to flow unobstructed into the hearts of people who have cleared their karma and opened their hearts.

People with open hearts that allow this flow of Love energy are going to raise the energetic manifesting ability of Earth.

As more people open their hearts, allowing Love to flow freely through them, the Earth will also experience a flowing of Love energy. When the Earth experiences free flowing Love energy, people will notice changes in Earth herself.

Your Earth will respond to this free-flowing Love energy with an abundance of miraculous changes.

As more and more people open their hearts and flow Love energy, your Earth will heal and return to a state of balance and beauty and luscious growth.

Your Earth will return to a state of Living that no one has witnessed in all of the history of mankind on Earth.

This free-flowing Love energy will allow Earth to return to a state of living humans have never witnessed.

Your Earth will return to her glorious and lush beginnings as a planet.

Living on planet Earth will be the wish of all beings in your Universe.

Living on planet Earth will be the biggest achievement possible.

Living on planet Earth will be openly linked to an honour of the highest regard in all of the Universe.

Once Earth returns to its perfect state of being, all beings in the Universe will wish to incarnate on Earth in order to witness the miracle of Love in person.

Earth will become a very popular place to incarnate and witness miracles on the planet of free-will.

Further to Earth becoming linked to high honour, the people who lived on Earth leading up to the Age of Aquarius will also be regarded with high honour.

These brave souls will be regarded with the highest possible honour in all of creation.

Prophecy 6

Received June 5, 2022

There is going to be an Event that Lightworkers will witness and others will not.

This Event will open the portal of Love to its fullest potential.

Before this Event, Lightworkers will notice changes in their manifestation abilities.

After this Event, Lightworkers will be blown away by their manifestation abilities.

This Event will open the hearts of Lightworkers allowing them to create the lives of their wildest dreams.

This Event will come after Lightworkers have healed their karma and completed their entanglements with others.

In other words, this Event will happen once Lightworkers have dealt with all their past and present life entanglements.

This Event will happen once the first wave of Lightworkers has completed this personal work.

This Event is going to be witnessed around the world by all Lightworkers who are ready to witness this Event.

Prophecy 7

Received June 6, 2022

People have been worrying about alien visits for a very long time. There is no need to worry.

When other beings show themselves to Earth beings it will only be for proper and honourable reasons.

Earth is a most well-known planet in the Universe and beyond.

Other beings are in awe of Earth and its people.

Many beings will try to incarnate on Earth. Those who cannot incarnate on Earth will try to at least visit somehow.

Many beings have already visited without being seen. Others have been seen. These beings are not a danger. These beings simply want to witness a bit of Earth's history and feel Earth's energy.

Life on Earth is unique and incredibly special.

When these visitors show themselves, it will create some chaos and many people will be afraid.

Lightworkers will hold an energy of peace and Love to help people find their balance again.

After this chaotic period, these visitors will bring information and technology to every person on Earth.

This is going to change life on Earth forever.

People will have their own source of food and energy and transportation.

This will shift the power on Earth away from a core group and spread it out to everyone equally. This will have repercussions that will benefit Earth and its people in ways no one could ever imagine.

Life on Earth will become peaceful and abundant.

Prophecy 8

Received June 6, 2022

People on Earth have always been infatuated with the stars.

People have been looking up to the stars for wisdom and direction since the beginning of humanity.

People have instinctually understood that the stars hold answers.

People have studied the stars, and their orbits, and motions, and planets, and learned a great deal.

There will be a new discovery in the stars. Knowledge of this new discovery will bring a lot of excitement to Earth and its people.

This new discovery will unlock a huge amount of new information.

This new discovery will give people a new outlook and help people understand their celestial home, and help people understand that there is so much more out there than anyone on Earth could ever imagine.

This new discovery is going to bring an incredible amount of new understandings with it.

This new discovery will change how people see the Universe and Earth's role in the Universe.

Prophecy 9

Received June 7, 2022

Miracles have a long history on Earth.

Miracles are somewhat misunderstood.

Some people think a miracle is a small wonderful thing.

Others think that a miracle is a big deal.

The miracles that are returning to Earth's experience are indeed big deals.

These miracles are going to blow away any small wondrous things.

These miracles are going to change lives completely.

These miracles are going to bring abundance, health and prosperity.

These miracles will become more and more common.

These miracles are going to have a life-changing affect on those who witness them.

These miracles are beginning now.

Prophecy 10

Received June 7, 2022

Happiness and Joy have been difficult for people to feel.

Before the Age of Aquarius, life was very challenging for most people.

The Age of Aquarius will change that.

This new age will bring a shift in the dominant emotions felt by Earth and its people.

As the Age of Aquarius unfolds, people will experience more and more Happiness and Joy.

Prophecy 11

Received June 7, 2022

In the beginning there was Light and that Light sparked bright and shot through the darkness to begin all of creation.

Since then, humanity has experienced a descent into darkness.

The Age of Aquarius is the beginning of humanity's ascent into the Light again.

Humanity came from a spark of Light and will now return to being a spark of Light without having to die and become pure Light.

Humanity's ascent into the Light will be a journey of 1000 years and because this journey is a long one, humanity deserves some encouragement along the way.

These prophecies are going to span 1000 years.

Once the early prophecies start unfolding, humanity will learn to trust these prophecies and that will bring a lot of encouragement to the world.

Prophecy 12

Received June 8, 2022

Once the portal of Love fully opens and begins free-flowing Love energy, Lightworkers will be rewarded for all their hard work.

Lightworkers are souls that have incarnated on Earth over and over again.

Lightworkers have experienced all the experiences possible for their soul's growth to elevate them to the status of Lightworker.

Every soul on Earth is on this journey to become a Lightworker.

Being a Lightworker simply means that you have had experiences on Earth that have led you to open your heart and mind to the Light.

Lightworkers are souls who are trying to live a life that encompasses the Light as much as possible.

There will be a mass awakening of the first wave of Lightworkers.

The Event will open the hearts of this first wave of Lightworkers all at the same time.

Prophecy 13

Received June 8, 2022

There are a few milestone events to watch for in the evolution of the Earth and its people.

Here are 5 events to watch for:

The first is the mass awakening of the first wave of Lightworkers, known as The Event. Once that has occurred and life has settled, there will be another wave of Lightworkers who awaken but not all at the same moment. The first wave of Lightworkers will help the second wave to awaken.

The second event to watch for is a visitation from beings who are not indigenous to Earth. These beings will bring knowledge and technology that will change the power dynamics on Earth forever.

The third event to watch for is a big one. This one will be witnessed by everyone on Earth. With all the commotion from the visitation and ensuing power rebalancing, people will need a bit of a distraction. This third event will provide that distraction. This third event will be a lot of fun. This third event will allow people from around the world to feel like they belong to a world that is compassionate and loving. This third event will be the creation of a new World Government that is truly and wholly loving.

The fourth event occurs a long time later. The fourth event will be the introduction of true space travel.

The last event to watch for is a huge graduation. Earth will eventually graduate to become a planet that is revered for its amazing transformation. Earth will graduate to become the first planet of free-will to make the transition from darkness to Light, and everyone who has ever incarnated on Earth will be honoured and respected. This graduation will elevate Earth to a status that no other world holds.

Prophecy 14

Received June 8, 2022

New and exciting things are in store for Earth and its people.

As people learn to flow Love energy through their hearts without restriction, there are going to be many pleasant side-effects.

People will begin to notice improved and unrestricted health.

People will notice easy manifestation abilities.

People will notice an increase in energy level and a decrease in need for sleep.

People will notice a craving for plant foods and a much reduced need to have any processed food.

People will also notice that they consume less food yet have more energy and health.

People will notice an ease of life in every aspect of life.

People will notice a connection with Nature that continues to grow and deepen.

People will notice a special ability to experience compassion for others. This compassion will help people to understand and appreciate the multitude of different journeys that are experienced by others.

People will notice a love feeling in their hearts almost always.

People will notice Hope gaining traction throughout the world.

People will notice a lifting of the fog and brightening of their futures.

People will notice that life has become a lot more fun.

People will notice that laughter is heard more often.

People will notice that their step is a little lighter, and their smile is a little brighter, and their eyes twinkle in the sunlight like never before.

Prophecy 15

Received June 9, 2022

Going forward, people on Earth are going to learn more about their unique place in the Universe.

Many different prophets will come forward with information about Earth's role in the Universe.

This information is going to be very surprising.

People on Earth tend to think they are unworthy and need a spiritual awakening before they can accept Love.

Love is available and deserved by every soul on Earth.

This is due to Earth's unique purpose.

The purpose of Earth is to graduate souls from a soul status to an Angel status.

Earth literally creates Angels.

Prophecy 16

Received June 9, 2022

Once people open their hearts to free-flowing Love energy unrestricted, lives are going to change.

This flow of unrestricted Love has never been available to people on Earth.

Earth was created to see if souls could find their way out of the darkness when given free-will to *not* do so.

Souls that came to Earth were the strongest and most respected souls in all of creation.

Even with the strongest and most respected souls coming to Earth, this experiment was never expected to succeed.

Earth has surprised all of creation.

Earth has indeed succeeded.

Earth has won the respect and honour of every being in all of creation.

Earth and its people have accomplished something incredible.

Now Earth and its people get to reap the rewards of all their hard work.

The Age of Aquarius is your reward.

Prophecy 17

Received June 9, 2022

Once Love becomes the dominant energy on Earth, this process of awakening will speed up.

The first wave of Lightworkers will awaken at the same moment.

They will be awakened by an Event.

After the first wave, there will be many, many, many more waves of Lightworkers, until eventually every soul on Earth is awakened and living their best life.

This process of awakening will occur over a period of almost 100 years.

Once everyone is awakened and living their best lives, then Earth truly enters the Age of Aquarius for everyone.

Lightworkers in the first wave are in for a big surprise very soon.

This mass awakening of the first wave of Lightworkers is going to be incredible.

The Event is a miracle in itself, but the experience of awakening together, at the same moment, will be what affects Lightworkers the most.

This awakening will be talked about for centuries to come.

Prophecy 18

Received June 9, 2022

Something amazing is in store for Earth and its people.

Once Love begins to flow unrestricted through your heart, you will experience a euphoria.

This euphoria will become your natural state of being.

Prophecy 19

Received June 9, 2022

Miracles are going to become more and more common, as more and more people open their hearts to flow Love energy unrestricted.

Love is what creates miracles.

Love is what creates.

Love is creation.

Lightworkers will become aware of their unique talents once they open their hearts to flowing Love energy unrestricted.

Lightworkers will remember who they truly are and all they have experienced in their many lives.

Lightworkers will then use their knowledge and talents to help the next wave of lightworkers to awaken.

Lightworkers in the first wave are going to open businesses and use their unique talents to help the following waves of lightworkers to awaken.

This is going to be a very exciting time for the first wave of lightworkers.

There will be a flurry of activity and anticipation of miracles and a feeling akin to childhood memories of Christmas Eve or Hanukkah or Diwali.

This feeling of excited anticipation is going to ripple around the world, and the next wave of lightworkers will feel this energy and it will bring them to the businesses opened by the first wave of lightworkers.

These businesses will become very successful.

Lightworkers around the world will finally start getting the recognition and respect that they deserve for all their hard work and talents.

Lightworkers, your time to shine is beginning.

Prophecy 20

Received June 9, 2022

Life on Earth will look very different in the next 100 years.

Once every soul on Earth is awakened, the energy of Earth will vibrate at a higher Love level than any other planet in the Universe. This will have some very pleasant side-effects.

Life will be happy and joyful for every person on Earth.

There will be no crime and no illness and no power imbalance. Everyone will be happy, healthy and independently powerful. People will have their own source of power and energy and life will be very pleasant.

People will pursue their own interests and share their talents freely with others.

People will spend their days exploring and learning and communing with others.

Earth will be returning to her luscious self and animals will be flourishing. People will invent new ways of living to benefit themselves and the plants and animals around them. People will live in harmony with their environment.

People will create symbiotic communities and live in groups of like-minded people who share common interests. Cities will become a thing of history. People will live in much smaller and much quieter communities.

Transportation from one community to another will be much different than it is today.

Prophecy 21

Received June 9, 2022

Crystals have been misunderstood on Earth.

Crystals are used by people to alter their energy, and help them attract prosperity and good health.

This is a fraction of what crystals can do.

Crystals carry a very special energy.

They can supply the Earth with more energy than it would ever need for an eternity.

Crystals are that powerful.

What crystals need in order to release their energy is Love.

Once people start flowing Love energy unrestricted, they will begin to discover how crystals can be used to create new and exciting lives.

Lightworkers who use crystals in their practices will be blown away by the power unleashed when they start flowing Love energy unrestricted.

Prophecy 22

Received June 10, 2022

Love is all powerful.

Love is a force of infinite possibilities.

Love is all of creation.

All of creation came from Love.

Every soul on Earth is all Love.

Every soul on Earth is an Angel or an Angel in the making.

Prophecy 23

Received June 10, 2022

Life on Earth has been a Light vs Dark atmosphere.

Everything on Earth comes from Love and then forgets all about Love.

People on Earth come from Love and are born onto Earth to try to remember their loving souls. In the process of trying to remember their loving souls, many people experience a lot of darkness. This journey is what life on Earth is all about. The journey from darkness to Light.

Now that Earth and its people have successfully made this journey and shown the Universe that it is possible, there is no more need to continue with trying to find the Light.

Now people on Earth can just live in the Light.

People will awaken to remember who they truly are, once they have each completed their journey to find the Light.

Everyone will complete their journeys at their own pace.

Over the next 100 years everyone on Earth will complete this journey, and then Earth will wholly be living in Light.

During this transition phase over the next 100 years, there are a few things to look forward to.

People on Earth will become more and more peaceful as more and more Light is anchored on Earth.

People will begin to invent things that are going to make life more fun and exciting.

People are going to be working less and playing more.

People will find true connections with others. These connections will be amongst their Soul Families and people will truly feel a sense of belonging.

People will learn that collaborating together creates an alchemy that far outweighs the benefits of working alone. These working collaborations will create many incredible inventions that will alter life on Earth forever.

People will learn how to work together and help others so that they too can awaken and live their best lives.

The atmosphere on Earth, as it transitions to the Light, will be an atmosphere of Love, connection and collaboration.

Prophecy 24

Received June 10, 2022

Having a premonition is a common experience on Earth by a select few people.

As people begin to flow Love energy unrestricted, they will also begin to have premonitions of the immediate future, and even some a bit further into the future. These premonitions are a side-effect of Love energy.

When people are attuned to Love energy, they are also attuned to all that is. All that is, is always connected on a Love energy level. When people are attuned to this Love energy level, they will experience premonitions that are like breadcrumbs leading to a desired outcome.

When a person is attuned to Love energy, the premonitions they receive will always give them insight as to an outcome that is desired. These premonitions can be used to help people help others head in the direction of their desired outcomes.

These premonitions can aid Lightworkers in helping others awaken.

These premonitions will give Lightworkers an idea of how they can help someone achieve their goals, and lead them in the direction of Love and Light.

Prophecy 25

Received June 10, 2022

Love energy will have a profound affect on the health and longevity of people.

Once people are flowing Love energy unrestricted, they will benefit from increased health and longevity.

People will be able to avoid disease and infection and benefit from a once-yearly fast of three days. This fast does not have to be difficult because people also have the Love energy to make the fasting easier.

The longevity of people will increase greatly over the next 100 years.

People will live longer and longer, reaching a maximum age of about 350 years.

This will not be a choice that everyone makes.

Once Earth and its people live wholly in the Love energy, there will be no death by disease or illness or infection.

Death will become a conscious choice.

People will decide when they are ready to return to the Light, and they will have beautiful ceremonies leading their loved ones into the Light.

Death will be a celebration of Love and Light.

Once people no longer die of disease, illness or infection they will become a witness to their own Return to the Light ceremonies.

No one will ever die alone unless they choose to, however, people will value their Soul Families so highly that they will always choose to have their families with them as they transition.

Prophecy 26

Received June 10, 2022

The weather is a big concern for many people on Earth.

The weather also is affected by the amount of Love energy anchored on Earth.

The worse the weather has been is in direct correlation with the amount of fear on Earth.

Fear creates weather events that create more fear.

Love creates weather that creates peace and more Love.

As more and more Love is anchored on Earth, people will see a direct affect on the weather.

Earth's weather and climate will both respond positively to Love energy.

Earth will balance herself and weather will be pleasant and climate will also become pleasant.

The extremes at the poles will disappear. The animals who live and survive in those extreme conditions will eventually leave Earth. Many people are worried about that.

As Earth balances and the extremes disappear, new animals will be able to come back to Earth.

There are many animals that had to leave Earth as her poles started to become extreme. Now those animals will have a chance to return, and people will have a chance to see this amazing wildlife that once existed on Earth.

The animals that will be leaving are very pleased that this is happening because it means that Earth and its people have succeeded in seeing the Light.

Earth will become luscious and full of wildlife from pole to pole.

The weather and climate will be pleasant and calm.

Earth will be full of joy and happiness from pole to pole.

Prophecy 27

Received June 11, 2022

Humankind has been through an incredible amount of pain and suffering.

The Age of Aquarius brings an end to the pain and suffering of humankind.

This new age is going to reward humankind for all their hard work.

People know this in their souls. People know that the end is near.

Some people misinterpret that to mean that the end of the world is near.

The imprint on your soul is that pain and suffering are ending.

This is a time to rejoice and give thanks as you move closer and closer to The Event that will get everything started.

Prophecy 28

Received June 11, 2022

Crystals have a secret.

Crystals hold a special energy that allows them to manifest anything on Earth.

In the hands of a person who is flowing Love energy unrestricted, and who understands the secret manifestation power of crystals, they literally become magic wands.

There are many Lightworkers in the first wave who have this knowledge and ability.

They will share this with others and magic will abound.

Prophecy 29

Received June 13, 2022

Lightworkers are already aware that when they break a trauma cycle, they are helping their ancestors to heal as well.

There is more happening that just that.

When a person heals a trauma or an addiction, they actually help to heal all trauma and addiction present on Earth at the time.

So, as Lightworkers begin to flow Love energy unrestricted and heal their bodies and lovingly feed their bodies, they will be helping everyone on Earth to do the same.

This ripple healing effect is strongest in those closest to the person who begins healing themselves.

This ripple healing effect opens a portal of healing energy around the Lightworker, and everyone the Lightworker encounters will benefit from this healing energy.

Some Lightworkers will be stronger than others with this ripple healing effect, but every Lightworker will radiate healing energy around them.

This healing energy is, of course, Love energy.

Some Lightworkers who are talented at radiating Love energy will experience a lot of miracles around them.

Their Love energy will radiate out strongly and people around them will be affected by the Love energy, and they will experience healing and wonderful manifestations in their lives.

So, Lightworkers will lead blessed lives and the people around them will also be blessed by the Love energy emitted.

So, Lightworkers will be surrounded by people who are healed, balanced, and blessed.

Lightworkers will be noticed for this effect.

Lightworkers will become very popular in social circles.

People will be attracted to the Love energy emitted by Lightworkers.

Lightworkers will need to be discerning about who they befriend.

Lightworkers do not need to feel pressure to befriend everyone.

Lightworkers have understandings of boundaries and will get a lot of practice with them.

Prophecy 30

Received June 13, 2022

Once people start flowing Love energy unrestricted, they will notice a few things:

Their health and prosperity will improve greatly.

Their relationships with others will also improve and become more meaningful.

They will become more and more youthful.

They will become more and more energetic.

They will become more and more intelligent.

They will become more and more happy.

They will become more and more psychic.

They will become more and more loving.

They will become more and more compassionate.

They will become more and more caring.

They will become more and more aware of the energy emitted by others.

They will become more and more giving.

They will become more and more spiritual.

They will become more and more grateful.

They will become more and more humble.

As people open up to flowing Love energy unrestricted, they will each go through this process of becoming their true selves.

Truly, each person on Earth is pure Love energy.

Prophecy 31

Received June 13, 2022

Just after the Earth and its people get used to flowing Love energy unrestricted, something incredible is going to happen, and this is going to open up many, many hearts and minds.

The Earth and its people know very little about the Universe.

Once everyone on Earth is flowing Love energy unrestricted, Earth will be invited into a council of the Universe.

This council governs all that is.

This council is a council of representatives from every enlightened planet in the Universe.

Love is the basis for this council.

All representatives come together in Love to help each other and understand each other. Earth will have a highly honoured place on this council.

One important role of this council is to ensure that planets that are not yet ready, do not receive information that will interrupt their natural development.

This council oversees all inter-planetary activity in the Universe.

This council is not a governing body nor does it rule over anyone. This council oversees the activities in the Universe and reports back to each planet that flows Love unrestricted. Everything is handled with Love unrestricted.

When Earth is invited to sit on this council, Earth and its people will be given information and knowledge that will change lives on Earth incredibly.

Prophecy 32

Received June 14, 2022

People on Earth have been experiencing a great divide.

This is going to continue for some time.

Lightworkers will awaken and begin to help other Lightworkers to awaken, and on the other side of the divide there may be chaos.

Lightworkers have done their work by the time they awaken, and they will be helping the subsequent waves of Lightworkers to complete their work in order to awaken.

People will notice that Lightworkers are happy and healthy and prosperous. This awareness of Lightworkers and their blessings will open the hearts and minds of those on the opposite side of the divide.

In this way, Lightworkers will be helping countless people simply by living their best lives.

Lightworkers will not help anyone by getting bogged down in the mud themselves.

Prophecy 33

Received June 14, 2022

The Age of Aquarius will bring many blessings to all the people on Earth.

This age will be the most prosperous and happy and healthy period Earth has ever seen.

People will be free to explore new areas and live a full and joyful life.

Joy is the energy associated with the Age of Aquarius. In contrast, healing was the keyword for the age of Earth's recent past.

There are a few exceptionally joyful things to look forward to in the Age of Aquarius:

People will be able to travel around the world in less than an hour.

People will be able to live anywhere on Earth and enjoy a pleasant climate and fantastic weather.

People will be able to have their own autonomy.

People will be able to live with their Soul Families and experience community like never before.

People will be able to love anyone without reservations.

People will feel a constant euphoria in their heart and soul.

People will be able to live a life filled with learning, and inventing, and problem-solving, and loving, and laughing, and playing.

Prophecy 34

Received June 14, 2022

This prophecy will be one of the last prophecies of the Age of Aquarius.

Near the end of the thousand-year Age of Aquarius, something incredible is going to occur.

After people have been living peacefully and prosperously for one thousand years, an incredible event will occur.

At that time, people will be very used to living almost as good as any life can possibly be. When people are used to a luxurious and peaceful life, they will start looking for more, and more, and more things to help them feel useful.

At that time, Earth will take on a new role in the Universe.

Earth and its people will become over-seers of a young planet that needs guidance. Earth and its people will guide this young planet and help the people to learn to flow Love energy unrestricted.

This planet will not be like Earth.

No other planet is like Earth.

This young planet will be much more aware of its birth in Light than Earth ever was, until the Age of Aquarius began.

Becoming a guide for this young planet will give Earth and its people something exciting and new to allow for continued growth and expansion of the soul.

Prophecy 35

Received June 14, 2022

Very big changes are in store for Earth and its people.

Some changes are physical, and some changes are experiential, and some changes are philosophical.

Some of the physical changes will not be felt at first. These physical changes will occur as a Lightworker is getting ready to awaken. Once the Lightworker has completed all their work, these behind-the-scenes physical changes will begin.

Some of these physical changes are as follows:

Lightworkers will open their hearts to a trickle of Love energy, and this will help them acclimate to the Love energy so that they don't become overwhelmed when flowing Love energy unrestricted.

Lightworkers will also experience a physical change to their cells as they prepare to flow Love energy unrestricted. This cellular change will not be felt or detected but must be complete before flowing Love energy unrestricted.

Finally, Lightworkers will begin living their lives from a basis of Love. A life lived from a basis of Love may experience some upheavals in the areas of job/career, partner/spouse and friends. These changes are all necessary to prepare the Lightworker for their new and blessed life.

Prophecy 36

Received June 14, 2022

No other planet is even close to being similar to Earth.

Earth is the only planet where people are born in darkness and have the free-will to explore and find their true beginnings in Light.

Every other planet is aware of its birth in Light and they strive to learn and grow in that knowing.

It is the darkness on Earth that makes it so unique.

Darkness is simply a lack of Light.

So, people on Earth are born into an energy that is not flowing Love unrestricted. Instead, the energy of Earth is an energy that is like a blank slate.

The energy of Earth was neither Light nor Dark when Earth was created. The experiment was to see if Angels and potential Angels could remember their beginnings in Light.

This experiment was never expected to succeed.

Similar experiments had been tried before and all failed to produce Light.

Earth is the first and only experiment of free-will to produce Light.

Earth shines so brightly in the Universe now with all the Light that it has created from a blank slate.

Earth is highly honoured because it is the only planet to ever produce Light from a blank slate.

All other planets start with Light and produce more Light. Earth started with nothing and has produced the most vibrant and bright Light in the Universe.

Every soul that has ever incarnated on Earth is responsible for this incredible success.

Every soul that has ever incarnated on Earth is celebrated and acknowledged throughout all that is.

Souls that have incarnated on Earth are given a special name badge.

Souls that have incarnated on Earth are called Light Makers and they are the most revered souls in all that is.

Prophecy 37

Received June 15, 2022

Right when things look bleakest is when an opportunity arrives.

The prospects of Earth were bleak for the last 2000 years.

People on Earth were having a challenging time seeing any Light and just as often they would act with malice.

In the last century and a half that started to shift dramatically.

People became more caring and understanding of others. People started to make choices based in Love and it changed the trajectory of Earth.

Once people started making choices from a basis of Love and Light, the Earth changed its path very quickly and dramatically.

In 1986 the Earth and its people passed a crucial tipping point and Love became the more dominant energy on Earth.

People may have noticed that things seem to have gotten worse since then.

The Earth was like a massive airplane in a high-speed dive, and in 1986 it woke up and yanked back on the controls to get out of the dive. Just like a massive airplane it will not respond immediately, and it will continue to lose altitude before the airplane finally stops descending and starts ascending. That is where Earth and its people are now.

Earth and its people have finally stopped descending and are now beginning to ascend.

This does not mean that everyone will be living a blessed life from here on. The process of learning to flow Love energy unrestricted will take 100 years to reach everyone on Earth.

In light of this information, a celebration is warranted.

Earth and its people have worked incredibly hard to accomplish something that was deemed impossible.

Everyone will eventually be celebrated.

In the meantime, a celebration is in store for the first wave of Lightworkers.

The Event that will awaken the first wave of Lightworkers is a huge gift to every Lightworker on Earth.

The Event is the birth of Love itself on Earth.

Prophecy 38

Received June 15, 2022

Once Love is born on Earth and people begin flowing Love energy unrestricted, life is going to become more and more joyful and creative.

Once people start flowing Love energy unrestricted, they will be connected to all that is, and they will receive creative ideas to help make life on Earth more and more fun and exciting.

Once people start flowing Love energy unrestricted, new inventions will open Earth to new experiences.

These inventions will bring clarity around the oceans and their animals, as well as a greater understanding of space and the planets and stars of the Universe.

These inventions will also bring a way of traveling that is faster than anything Earth has seen and does not use conventional fuels.

These inventions will also allow people to just have more fun and spend their leisure time doing exciting activities.

People will begin to spend more time outside again and really connect with each other.

Prophecy 39

Received June 15, 2022

Fostering a life with Light is one talent that Lightworkers have.

Lightworkers lend their Light to others so that they can accelerate their growth.

Everyone on Earth is going to awaken no matter what happens from here on.

The role of Lightworkers is to help accelerate that process.

Once a Lightworker flows Love energy unrestricted, they will discover their special talents and they can use these talents to help others awaken faster.

This means that no Lightworker is above another.

All people on Earth will become Lightworkers and will awaken without any help.

Helping others is a choice based in Love to help Earth and its people flow Love energy unrestricted as soon as possible.

Prophecy 40

Received June 15, 2022

One very big surprise is in store for the first wave of Lightworkers.

It will become a major Event in their lives.

The Event will bring so many changes and blessings to Lightworkers in the first wave.

This is something these Lightworkers have earned.

These Lightworkers have done their personal work and cleared all their karma, and they did most of this work on their own in a time when this spiritual practice was not accepted.

These Warriors of Light deserve this gift of Love.

Prophecy 41

Received June 15, 2022

Nature is a sanctuary for many people, however, they don't fully realize the power that Nature has.

The plant and animal life on Earth have an energy of pure Love.

People go out into Nature to feel better and recharge. This is because of the Love energy emitted by plants and animals. People can feel this Love energy and they feel better after being around this energy.

Plants and animals on Earth carry this Love energy, and have been helping people feel and see this Love energy since the beginning of people on Earth. Once people are flowing Love energy unrestricted, they will notice a huge difference when they connect with plants or animals.

Being able to flow Love energy unrestricted will allow people to feel the true power of the Love energy emitted by plants and animals.

People will want to spend even more time in Nature and with animals.

People will feel amazing when in Nature and with animals.

Prophecy 42

Received June 15, 2022

The wind on Earth plays a special role.

The wind is also an energy of Love.

The wind can help cleanse a person's aura.

Being outside in the wind helps people clear their energy field and feel better.

People who are attracted to sports where the wind blows around them, such as running, and sailing, and water-skiing, and many others, are really seeking out a fun way to keep their energy clean and balanced.

The wind is a blessing and a curse.

Too much wind is a curse. Too much wind is caused by an imbalance in the energy of Earth herself. Earth also gets imbalanced and needs a clearing wind every once in a while.

As more people begin to flow Love energy unrestricted, there will be less and less need for excessive winds to clear Earth's energy field.

Prophecy 43

Received June 15, 2022

This prophecy will be fulfilled near the end of the Age of Aquarius.

The Earth and its people will not ever need to die again.

By the end of the Age of Aquarius, the Earth and its people will graduate to become a planet of all dimensions.

As a planet of all dimensions, people will be able to come and go from Earth without having to die.

People will be able to access Earth whenever they wish, and leave Earth whenever they wish to be in other dimensions without having to die.

This is difficult for people on Earth now to fully comprehend. It is not necessary to fully comprehend this prophecy.

The message of this prophecy is that people on Earth will eventually reach a point where they no longer have to die and be reborn in order to come to Earth or to leave Earth.

Earth will be a part of what people on Earth now refer to as Heaven.

Prophecy 44

Received June 15, 2022

There are so many hidden treasures on Earth that are yet to be discovered.

Treasures like the Love energy in all plants and animals.

Earth is full of treasures like that.

Love energy is hidden in plain sight everywhere.

People are fond of honeybees because honeybees are tiny, flying, portals of Love energy. For their size, they carry more Love energy than anyone would ever expect.

Penguins have a similar effect. The poles are extreme in climate and therefore they need extra Love to balance them and prevent even faster extreme climate development. Penguins hold a lot more Love energy than anyone would imagine.

Polar Bears are the same. These animals have a special purpose to hold that Love energy and balance the extremes of the poles. Soon they will not be needed as much and their numbers will naturally decline.

Another treasure is the dragonfly. Dragonflies are revered by people who intuitively understand their importance. Dragonflies hold a tremendous amount of Love energy. Also, they eat mosquitos and mosquitos are a representation of energy at the opposite end of the scale from Love.

This energy on Earth is represented by mosquitos and people will notice that mosquitos and other biting insects of that sort will decrease in number as more and more people flow Love energy unrestricted.

Birds and other insect-eating animals will be able to survive on non-biting insects and new insect species that will replace the mosquito as they leave. The new insects will be aware of their beginnings in Light and they will be of humble service to Earth and its animals.

Earth is an incredible planet full of hidden treasures.

Prophecy 45

Received June 16, 2022

Addiction is something that is affecting a phenomenal portion of Earth's population at this time.

There are several Lightworkers who are working very hard to overcome this affliction.

These Lightworkers are healing this condition for more than just themselves.

These Lightworkers are healing their addictions so that the healing energy is present and strong on Earth.

Once the few, strong, Lightworkers have accomplished this healing, the healing energy will be anchored to Earth for others to access more easily.

These Lightworkers are doing very difficult and incredible work.

The addiction crisis on Earth is about to change.

The addiction crisis on Earth may be one of the most difficult energies to live with.

These Lightworkers, that have been working through their own addictions, will make it much easier for others once they anchor the healing energy.

Lightworkers have been working to heal many, many, many different issues, anchoring that healing energy for others to access.

Lightworkers truly are Light Workers.

Prophecy 46

Received June 16, 2022

The Event is going to change the lives of the first wave of Lightworkers in unimaginable ways.

These Lightworkers will need time to adjust to their new reality.

Lightworkers deserve this gift of time.

Prophecy 47

Received June 17, 2022

This is a prophecy about the history of Earth.

Earth was born in an energy of a blank slate.

Earth was given the free-will to become Light or not.

Earth was born with a lot of violent energy.

This violent energy was needed to literally create the ball of molten lava that is at the core of Earth.

Without this violence, Earth would not exist.

Through a series of further violent events, the landscape of Earth was formed.

Then, energies started inhabiting the Earth and these energies were born in violence.

This was Earth's energy for a very long time. Earth was thought to be another failed attempt to create Light from a blank slate.

Then a miracle happened.

One soul on Earth began to see Light where others did not.

Soon, that soul showed others the Light, and they showed others, and they showed others. In a short time, Earth's energy started to shift from violence to Love.

That first opening to Love was a miracle.

Now Earth is about to experience Love being born on Earth.

Birth has been a violent and painful experience.

This will change.

With Love being born, birth will embrace Love.

Birth will abandon its violent and painful past and embrace a loving and peaceful new beginning.

Birth on Earth will become a loving and peaceful event for every woman over the next 100 years.

Prophecy 48

Received June 17, 2022

On an ordinary day, Love will be born on Earth.

This day will not be special in any other way.

Love will be born on Earth and change the energy of Earth forever.

Love will not be born in violence and pain.

Love will be born on Earth, in Love, and peace, and euphoria.

Once Love arrives, the first wave of Lightworkers will feel this energy and it will gently awaken them.

This mass awakening will occur in the hours and days following Love's arrival. This will unfold over a day or so because Lightworkers are happy to awaken in their own best time.

This awakening will be gentle, and peaceful, and life-changing.

Lightworkers will be delighted and joyful beyond their imagination.

Lightworkers will need time to absorb and adjust to their new reality.

Lightworkers will receive a lot of information upon awakening, and will be excited to begin helping others.

The gift of time to adjust is the best gift a Lightworker can give themselves upon awakening.

Prophecy 49

Received June 19, 2022

The Light on Earth has been growing at a steady rate since the tipping point in 1986.

The Light will continue to grow and will start to grow faster and faster making it easier and easier to see the Light, and feel the Light, and embody the Light.

The more Light there is on Earth, the easier it is for people to complete their karma.

Some people think that karma is a punishment for perceived bad behaviour.

Karma is actually unfinished business.

This karma can arise from past lives and can also be created in a current life.

This karma is a result of an experience that was not experienced fully. For example, if someone is betrayed by a partner, they need to process that experience and feel the feelings. If they instead, push away their feelings and make attempts to forget the experience, they will create karma.

This karma will come back later in their life to be experienced properly, or they will carry it into their next life and will experience a betrayal again in order to give them the opportunity to feel it and heal it.

This experience of bringing past life karma into a new life is the choice of each individual soul. Souls choose to do this because clearing karma is what allows a soul to grow, and learn, and create Light.

Karma is one way that a soul creates Light.

Feeling is healing and healing is Light-creating.

Prophecy 50

Received June 19, 2022

This prophecy is one of the wildest in this collection.

Right now, people are living their lives and trying to get through each day with a bit of grace and sanity.

Soon, this will be a distant memory for most people on Earth.

Life is going to change for everyone, once Love is born.

People will become disillusioned with working for a living and they will find ways to free themselves of this paradigm. People will begin to live instead of working until they die.

People will become more creative about how to offer help to others, and will be given blessings for their talents. These blessings will allow them to live without needing to work at a job they dislike.

This will be available to everyone on Earth, once Love is born, not just Lightworkers.

People will be rewarded for helping others, and this experience will help them to see, and feel, and embrace the Light.

Prophecy 51

Received June 20, 2022

Open hearts are essential for flowing Love energy unrestricted.

It is the work of Lightworkers to open their hearts in order to accept this flow of Love energy, unrestricted. Lightworkers open their hearts by seeing the Light and clearing their karma.

No one is born with an open heart on Earth but soon that will change.

Once Love is born on Earth, then people will begin being born with an open heart. Not everyone will be born with an open heart. Many souls will still choose to come in with karma to clear and heal to earn their open heart.

Opening hearts is what Lightworkers will help others to do.

People open their hearts as they see the Light on Earth. Lightworkers will shine their Light brightly for others to see and feel. Lightworkers, living their best lives, is what will help others to see the Light.

The best thing a Lightworker can do is to simply live their best life.

Helping others with their talents, is actually a secondary way to help others.

Karma-clearing is what Lightworkers will do with their talents, and Light-awareness is what Lightworkers will do with their best-lives-lived.

Giving others an awareness of Light in the darkness is more of a gift than anyone on Earth realizes.

Holding steady and shining your Light brightly is *THE* most powerful thing any Lightworker can do.

Prophecy 52

Received June 20, 2022

Forgetting that you are Light is an incredibly difficult path to choose.

People who incarnate on Earth have chosen this path over and over again. This experience is incredibly challenging, and has been tried many times and failed.

Earth is the first and only planet to succeed in feeling and seeing the Light.

It cannot be expressed enough that Earth and its people have accomplished something miraculous, and incredible, and phenomenal.

The people on Earth are currently being celebrated around the Universe.

Having anything to do with Earth, now makes you an instant Universal Celebrity.

People on Earth are being celebrated yet they are unaware of this happening, and they are still suffering through their karma and not seeing the Light it creates.

This is difficult for people on Earth to condone.

The Universe understands that all will unfold well from now on, and must let it unfold naturally.

People on Earth, who awaken to the Light, will have more difficulty understanding that all will unfold well from this point, and it must unfold naturally.

People who awaken will want to save everyone immediately, and that is just not possible.

Awakening is a personal process and must happen naturally for each individual.

Lightworkers can help speed up the process for some, however, they cannot make someone ready if they are not ready.

Prophecy 53

Received June 20, 2022

Hope is a very strong attractor of Light.

Light is a result of Hope.

One of the gifts of a Lightworker living their best life is to give Hope to others.

When people see others succeeding, they can either feel Hope that life can become better for them, or they can become jealous and not see or feel any Light.

How different people react is their own journey and has nothing to do with the Lightworker.

Hope is much stronger than anyone on Earth realizes.

Boosting Hope is a very valid way to make Light.

Hope leads to Light every single time.

Hope can be dashed, and that may be difficult for some to experience, however, the Light made from that Hope is everlasting.

Prophecy 54

Received June 20, 2022

Once Love is born on Earth, many blessings will occur around the world.

Lightworkers will be blessed with many things.

They will make a lot of Light in enjoying these blessings.

Others will notice their blessings and react according to their own personal journeys.

Those that react with Hope for their own lives will create Light in their own lives, and this Light will bring them blessings too.

In this way a Lightworker can help many others by just living their lives.

Prophecy 55

Received June 22, 2022

Life on Earth is about to change in ways that no one can presently imagine.

In the next 100 years, there will be very little left of what currently exists on Earth.

People will dismantle a lot of what presently exists on Earth. This dismantling will occur over time and will be gentle, and loving, and considerate of those who rely on these old systems and buildings.

Life on Earth will look very, very, very different in 100 years. Cities are going to slowly disappear and people will relocate to more personalized communities.

These personalized communities will live in harmony with each other, and share many values that make living in community much more pleasant.

Each community will be unique, and will have a role to play in the larger area around them.

A network of communities will make up a larger community, and a wholistic approach to life will be conceivable with this community network around each individual community.

Life in these personalized communities will be very fulfilling, and the bonds that people will have with each other will be stronger and better than any friendship bonds people have experienced on Earth before.

Prophecy 56

Received June 22, 2022

Going a bit deeper into these communities will reveal something special.

Each community will consist of a Soul Family.

A Soul Family is a group of souls that have done a lot of work together, and have grown together and learned together.

These Soul Families are connected very deeply.

These Soul Families are going to change how people live in harmony with each other.

These Soul Families have so much experience being together, that living in harmony with each other is effortless and extremely rewarding.

These Soul Families will begin finding each other once Love flows unrestricted.

Prophecy 57

Received June 22, 2022

Jobs are going to change drastically over the next 100 years.

People are going to need less food, and new ways of traveling are going to change many jobs around the world.

Power is another area that will be dismantled. Every person on Earth will be able to create their own power and have autonomy.

These few changes will alter the jobs available drastically.

There will also be changes to the manufacturing industry and the industrial industry. Most jobs will be focused around services, and a few other areas that will change, but will still create jobs. The manufacturing industry will change greatly, and it will still create jobs, however, these jobs will be much more rewarding than they are today.

The travel industry is going to thrive. Everyone on Earth will have access to a mode of transportation that they can power autonomously. This is going to allow people to travel freely, wherever they desire.

So, jobs are going to shift to become more service oriented.

People are going to get very creative with their services, and with inventing new things to entertain and bring joy to others.

The number of hours that people spend at their jobs is also going to change drastically. People will be able to earn a proper living while working less hours than they do now.

Life is going to become more about leisure time and less about work time.

Prophecy 58

Received June 22, 2022

Life on Earth is going to become a lot more fun and exciting.

One area that is going to create a lot of excitement is the area of space travel.

Space travel is a very distant acquisition for Earth, however, the journey to get there is going to create a lot of excitement for a lot of people on Earth.

The journey to get space travel on Earth is going to involve a lot of teachings from beings around the Universe.

These beings are going to share their space travel knowledge over the span of about 250 years.

Prophecy 59

Received June 22, 2022

On the journey to space travel, people on Earth must first learn more about the Universe and its people.

This is what is going to create so much excitement over the years leading up to space travel.

Learning about the other beings in the Universe is going to be an experience like nothing ever before.

This has literally never happened before.

There has never been a planet of free-will that has succeeded until Earth succeeded.

The prospect of teaching the people of Earth all about the mysteries of the Universe is an exciting and joyful one.

The beings around the Universe are already preparing to make contact and start sharing their knowledge.

Prophecy 60

Received June 23, 2022

For the lives of Lightworkers to change and become blessed, they must do their personal work first.

This personal work is what people came to Earth to do.

This personal work is what being human is all about.

This personal work is not easy.

This personal work involves experiences like addiction, betrayal, assault, phobias, molestation, abuse, and many other difficult and terrifying experiences.

This personal work involves healing these experiences, and justifying your anger means you have not yet healed that experience. Once an experience has been healed completely, there is no residue anger or sadness or fear.

This is the work that Lightworkers do.

This personal work is incredibly difficult.

This personal work is what Lightworkers will be helping the next waves of Lightworkers to do.

Everyone can manage their own healing on their own.

Lightworkers simply help to speed up the process and even make it a bit easier, by holding space with the person healing themselves.

Lightworkers can help ease the pain quite a bit, however, this can only happen if the person healing allows the Lightworker to help.

This requires a lot of trust and many people requiring healing have a difficult time with trust.

This personal work is a big job and Earth and its people are doing it like never before.

Prophecy 61

Received June 23, 2022

Eating and the food people eat is going to change drastically.

As people flow Love energy unrestricted, they will need much less food and they will become a lot more energetic.

The food that people consume now, actually keeps people somewhat lethargic.

As people flow Love energy unrestricted, they will choose to eat fresh fruits, and vegetables, and nuts, and seeds, and legumes, and a few choice grains. This diet will provide more energy than people can imagine, and people who are needing more energy will become clean eaters to get more energy.

People will also eat much less food.

The human body needs Light energy to survive and plant foods give you that energy.

Love energy is also Light energy.

So, once people flow Love energy unrestricted, they will require very little food to remain energetic and healthy.

Water is also important for people to drink. Other drinks will be left behind in favour of water and tea.

Once people flow Love energy unrestricted, they will eat a bit of plant food and drink a few glasses of water, and be more energetic and healthier than ever before.

Prophecy 62

Received June 24, 2022

Once people flow Love energy unrestricted, there will be many blessings that are unexpected.

One of these blessings will involve people's relationship with animals.

Love is going to change every relationship each person has, including their relationship with animals.

All animals are Light energy and they respond to other Light energies.

Once people flow Love energy unrestricted, they will become beacons of Light.

Animals will feel this Light energy and they will befriend those people. Domestic and wild animals alike will be drawn to people who are emitting this Light energy.

People will notice that animals show themselves, and even become friends with people who flow Love energy unrestricted.

These free-flowing people are going to be able to have wild animal friends, and it will be extremely rewarding for them.

Prophecy 63

Received June 24, 2022

Reality is a personal experience.

Everyone on Earth is experiencing a different reality.

There is no such thing as one truth.

Reality is a construct of each person's experiences.

What is real and truthful for one person is a complete lie for another.

This can cause misunderstandings and confusion. This has also caused many, many, many wars on Earth.

As people flow Love energy unrestricted, they will become aware of the realities of different people, and they will be able to find solutions that will benefit all the different realities.

As more and more people awaken and flow Love energy unrestricted, there will be fewer and fewer conflicts around the world.

New and exciting realities are going to become available to people as they flow Love energy unrestricted.

These people will be able to create a reality for themselves that will be unbelievable and undetectable to others who are not flowing Love energy unrestricted.

Prophecy 64

Received June 25, 2022

This new reality, that Lightworkers will create once they flow Love energy unrestricted, will be a huge blessing.

Lightworkers will be able to create a space for themselves, where they can gather and experience soul connections like never before experienced on Earth.

Lightworkers will also be able to travel to this gathering space with ease.

Lightworkers are going to love spending time in this gathering space.

Prophecy 65

Received June 25, 2022

Right now, Lightworkers are looking forward to when these prophesies will begin.

Hope is a wonderful catalyst to bring these prophesies closer to fruition.

The more Hope that is generated, among Lightworkers in particular, the faster these events will begin to unfold.

Lightworkers must do their personal work and that cannot be skipped.

However, Lightworkers can also be hopeful, and that hopefulness creates Light, that will then help the other Lightworkers and themselves to complete their personal work faster.

Prophecy 66

Received June 25, 2022

This new reality that Lightworkers will create will also contain a knowledge library.

This knowledge library will be accessible to every person flowing Love energy unrestricted.

This knowledge library will remind Lightworkers of the possible lifetimes they are going to be able to live after this lifetime.

This knowledge library will also contain all the knowledge and information from each Lightworker's past lives.

This knowledge library is also known as The Akashic Records.

Lightworkers will have access to these records.

Lightworkers will be able to use the information contained in these records to help others complete their personal work.

Some Lightworkers have been able to access these records already, however, once they flow Love energy unrestricted, they will have access to every record in the library.

Prophecy 67

Received June 25, 2022

No one on Earth has always been on Earth.

Every soul on Earth has been somewhere else before Earth.

Many souls have experienced other planets of free-will, and have experienced their failure.

This failure is a strong energy that still resides in their cells.

Many people are going to need a lot of help to clear the karma of this failure.

This failure karma is a strong and difficult karma to clear.

This failure karma did not originate on Earth but these souls still have that energy as part of their soul. Therefore, this failure karma still must be cleared, even though it is not an energy that originated on Earth.

This is going to be a main theme in many people who are going to seek help from Lightworkers who are part of the first wave.

These Lightworkers have already healed their failure karma and they will be a great resource for others who are looking for help.

This failure karma is a big soul theme and it is one of the reasons that Earth was never thought to succeed.

This failure karma is also why Earth is so revered in its success.

Souls clearing this failure karma from their souls will have a huge effect on the Universe itself. This failure energy has been part of the Universe since the beginning of time.

When this failure energy is healed and released fully, the Universe will undergo a massive shift.

This massive shift is going to affect every being, and every planet, and every star, and every piece of matter in the Universe.

Prophecy 68

Received June 25, 2022

People on Earth like to think of themselves as new and improved over past generations of people on Earth.

In some ways this is true, and in other ways this is not true.

It took many millennia to get to this point in human history.

During that time, people went from being relatively aware of a bigger oneness to everything, and descended into a lonely existence, separate from everything and everyone.

This has not been an improvement.

People living on Earth today don't realize how past generations have been much closer to each other, and much happier.

Connection with others will increase anyone's happiness.

Disconnection with others will increase anyone's loneliness and depression.

Connection is a key component of being human and experiencing joy. Humans are hard-wired to enjoy each other's company.

The people living on Earth today have become used to being alone.

People living on Earth today will be surprised by the joy they feel when they start truly connecting with others, and genuinely feeling like they belong in a family group.

Prophecy 69

Received June 25, 2022

Having almost not succeeded makes the success of Earth even more sweet.

This success is a much bigger deal than anyone on Earth realizes.

Watching Earth these last few millennia has been a wild experience.

The other planets in the Universe were convinced of Earth's demise. Now, these planets are in a flurry of activity in order to prepare to educate the people of Earth.

Now that Earth has succeeded, and is on track for their first visitation, all the Universe is watching again.

This visitation will be very gentle and loving, and many people are going to be extremely excited.

Others will be extremely afraid, however, that will be a small portion of Earth's population.

This initial visitation will be done by the children of a very advanced planet in the Universe. These children will appear around the world and give people the message of their arrival.

These children are Light energy as never seen on Earth.

Those people on Earth who are awake, and even those who are not but can feel energy, will feel the impressive Love energy from these children. Once the children have made contact, and people are feeling more comfortable, then the adults will start arriving.

This is going to be extremely exciting for many people on Earth.

The adults have the same feel, and they also have a lot of knowledge to share. This knowledge will be shared with every person on Earth, and every person on Earth will have access to the knowledge and technology shared.

This will occur over a few years.

This first visitation will be the slowest and longest. Subsequent visitations will occur faster, and will be more individually based and less world wide.

There will be many, many, many visitations.

Prophecy 70

Received June 27, 2022

Sometime in the next 100 years, a miracle will occur.

This miracle will be seen around the world.

This miracle will be given to Earth and its people when the majority of people are flowing Love energy unrestricted.

This miracle will involve a new way to travel.

This new way to travel will allow people to travel around the world in less than one hour.

This new way to travel will become a part of everyone's personal belongings.

This new way to travel will be accessible by everyone, even those who have not awakened yet.

This new way to travel will open the world up for everyone to explore and experience joy.

This new way to travel will bring joy because it will allow people to visit anyone they wish, in places that are normally too far away to be in touch regularly.

This new way to travel will allow people to stay in touch with their beloved family and friends who live in various places around the world.

Prophecy 71

Received June 27, 2022

Right now, there are no people on Earth who are flowing Love energy unrestricted.

This Love energy unrestricted will only be available once the Love portal opens. This will happen at the same time as The Event.

Once The Event happens, it will trigger the mass awakening of the first wave of Lightworkers, by opening a portal of Love.

This first wave of Lightworkers will have completed their personal work and opened their hearts so that when the portal of Love opens, they will be able to flow Love energy unrestricted through their open hearts.

This Event is a birth of Love on Earth, and this birth of Love will open the portal of Love.

This birth is a one-time Event that will alter birth on Earth forever.

This birth will not cause pain.

Instead, this birth will be accompanied by a strong experience of joy and euphoria. After this birth in joy and euphoria, other births will begin to arrive in joy and euphoria.

Over the course of many years, eventually all births on Earth will arrive in joy and euphoria.

Prophecy 72

Received June 27, 2022

For Love to be born on Earth, there had to first be an Earth.

Earth was first born in the energy of a blank slate and soon descended into violence and brutality. However, this violence and brutality is what created the Earth, and allowed it to support a human race.

Now, Earth and its people have risen from their violent and brutal beginnings, and they are creating a new beginning.

Earth is beginning anew.

Earth is being born in Love.

Earth is being born in Love without having to die first.

This is unprecedented.

This is a huge deal.

Earth is being born in Love after descending into violence and brutality.

Earth has accomplished something incredible.

This birth in Love is Earth's gift for accomplishing something incredible.

This birth in Love is a huge gift, and Earth and its people deserve every blessing that will come from this birth in Love.

Prophecy 73

Received June 27, 2022

There is one more very important message about The Event.

This Event will be felt and psychically seen by the first wave of Lightworkers.

These Lightworkers will understand the importance of The Event.

Others will have no clue that anything special happened.

Lightworkers will have a secret that no one else knows.

This shared experience will bring this first wave of Lightworkers closer than ever.

These Lightworkers will be able to recognize each other as they go about their days.

Prophecy 74

Received June 27, 2022

Time is a relative interpretation of each person's experience on Earth.

Time can feel short and time can feel long.

People on Earth don't understand time the way others in the Universe understand time.

As people on Earth flow Love energy unrestricted, time will become irrelevant for them. People flowing Love energy unrestricted will experience time as others in the Universe experience time.

This will open up many exciting possibilities.

People who flow Love energy unrestricted will be able to observe different times in Earth's history, and witness the ups and downs of humanity.

Prophecy 75

Received June 27, 2022

Once people flow Love energy unrestricted, they will have access to all of Earth's history, and they will be able to look at different times in order to learn about Earth and its people.

This ability to see through time will be very exciting, and Lightworkers will spend many hours observing history for themselves.

Prophecy 76

Received June 28, 2022

When people flow Love energy unrestricted, a lot of things will open up to Love.

People will have access to things they never knew existed. Some of these things are small and some are life-changing.

These are some of the things that will open up to Love:

People will be able to feel each other's energy like never before.

People will understand each other's realities.

People will recognize others who are flowing Love energy unrestricted.

People will become happier and more joyful.

People will become more observant.

People will become a lot smarter.

People will become kind and understanding.

People will become friendlier and more caring.

People will become lighter in weight and begin to emit a soft glow.

People will become healthy and strong.

People will become taller.

People will become faster at everything they do.

People will become manifesting masters.

People will become Light Workers and Light Emitters.

Prophecy 77

Received June 28, 2022

Once the world has been through its first visitation from beings in the Universe, this awakening process will pick up speed.

Just as the people are settling in with their new knowledge and technology, everything will change again.

The next big change will be in the making of a new World Government.

This new World Government will consist of all members who are flowing Love energy unrestricted.

So, this new World Government will be loving and gentle and open to harmony in the world.

This new World Government will change life on Earth in ways that cannot be imagined now.

This new World Government will bring everyone on Earth together as one beautiful race.

Prophecy 78

Received June 28, 2022

In the far, distant, future of Earth and its people, there will come a time when Earth will be a very popular tourist destination for others in the Universe.

When visitors come from elsewhere in the Universe, they have access to all of Earth's history because they understand time differently.

This makes Earth an incredible tourist destination because others in the Universe are fascinated by Earth's progression from violence and brutality to Love and Joy.

These visitors will come to observe and feel Earth's energy through time.

These visitors will interact with Earth and its people when they visit.

People on Earth will cherish their time and interactions with these visitors.

These visitors will always bring something with them to share in exchange for their visit.

These gifts will be bestowed on the people of Earth and bring lots of joy and happiness.

Prophecy 79

Received June 28, 2022

Money is something that everyone on earth strives for.

Money is simply a physical manifestation of energy.

Money is energy.

Love is energy.

Love is the strongest energy there is.

Once people flow Love energy unrestricted, the striving for money will disappear.

The people who flow Love energy unrestricted, will be able to create fantastic lives without money and without striving.

People who flow Love energy unrestricted, will have manifestation abilities that surpass anything seen on Earth.

Money will also begin to have less and less value to people as the Earth evolves.

People will instead help each other and receive help from each other, freely and with Love.

This will unfold over the next 90 years.

Prophecy 80

Received June 28, 2022

Right now, there are people who believe the world is about to end.

These people are remembering a time when they incarnated on a planet of free-will that did not succeed.

This feeling of doom is incredibly strong in some people.

These people will be very forceful with their opinions and trying to convince others of Earth's demise.

Everyone on Earth has their own guidance from their own team of Angels and Guides. These Guides are specific to each person and most have been with that person for all their lifetimes on Earth.

When a person hears something that is not in their best interest, their Angels and Guides give them signs to help them make decisions.

One of these signs is a feeling of uncomfortableness.

When someone hears something that is not in their best interest, they will feel uncomfortable. This is how your Angels and Guides guide you.

When you hear something that *is* in your best interest, you will feel peace and joy.

Discernment is learning to heed these feelings and make your own best decisions.

What is best for one person will not be best for all people.

So, two people can hear the same thing and one person feels joy while the other feels uncomfortable.

They are both correct.

They will each be best to follow that guidance and make their own decisions that are best for them individually.

Prophecy 81

Received June 28, 2022

Something magical is about to happen.

Right now, Earth and its people are sleeping soundly.

The Love energy on its way to Earth is smiling quietly.

The people on Earth are unaware of the beautiful changes about to occur.

This is a precious time full of possibilities.

This is the Love energy's favourite moment. The moment before Love arrives is a special time.

This is the time where the people of Earth are still asleep and have no idea that everything is about to change. They have no idea how incredible and blessed they are.

This is indeed a special moment for the Love energy.

Love is on her way, and she is smiling quietly because she knows what is about to happen.

Prophecy 82

Received June 28, 2022

Now and again, there is a person on Earth who brings forth a lot of followers.

These people have a shared energetic imprint, and so when a strong person with that imprint becomes a leader, others with that imprint follow them. This has occurred over and over again on Earth.

This has often caused violence and brutality as the strong leader frees a sense of belonging and power within those who follow that leader.

As Earth evolves, there will emerge a few people who are going to play out their karma in big ways. These people will appear as leaders and many will follow them because of their own karmic imprints.

This may feel and seem chaotic.

However, this karma being played out on such a grand scale is actually helping Earth to evolve faster.

This grand scale karmic release will create a lot of healing and ready people for their own awakening.

This chaotic period is actually a blessing to help speed up the awakening process.

Prophecy 83

Received June 28, 2022

There is something that people can do during these chaotic periods on Earth.

People can focus on Love and completely ignore the chaos as much as possible.

Some people will feel compelled to join in the chaos to varying degrees and that is their path.

However, many people will be able to just carry on with their lives and that is the best thing they can do to help Earth evolve.

The only other thing people can do to help is to send Love and Light to the chaos.

Prophecy 84

Received June 28, 2022

Once people flow Love energy unrestricted, people will notice that their lives are changing.

People will notice that one day Lightworkers were just a bit *out there,* and the next day Lightworkers were living their best lives.

People will notice the blessings bestowed upon Lightworkers, and they will wonder what is going on.

People who have not been aware of their own journeys will suddenly see their path and want to make changes.

People will ask Lightworkers many questions about their journeys.

People will seek out the help of various Lightworkers to help them open their hearts.

Lightworkers will become honoured and respected.

Prophecy 85

Received June 28, 2022

In the not-too-distant-future, something surprising will occur.

As the energy on Earth begins to shift, as more and more Lightworkers flow Love energy unrestricted, something surprising will occur.

People who have been sound asleep with no hint of waking, will begin to question everything.

These people will be the most satisfying people for Lightworkers to work with.

These are the people who felt a bit lost in the darkness.

These are people that others would never imagine could ever see the Light.

So, when these people begin to awaken, Lightworkers will gain a lot of satisfaction and Love energy from helping these people see their Light.

Prophecy 86

Received June 28, 2022

Helping someone see their own Light is incredibly satisfying.

Lightworkers in the first few waves are generally aware of their own Light, so helping them is wonderful but not as satisfying as helping someone who does not see their own Light.

Helping someone see their own Light is a wonderful thing.

There is no way to describe the energy that is created and released when someone in the darkness finally sees their own Light.

This will become a treasured experience for all Lightworkers.

Prophecy 87

Received June 29, 2022

There is one happy-go-lucky person in every person on Earth.

Everyone on Earth has a happy-go-lucky side.

Some people are really good at concealing this side of themselves.

As the energy on Earth begins to shift, people will begin showing their happy-go-lucky side, despite themselves.

People will feel this energy shift in their souls, even if they are not aware of it, and they will not be able to stop themselves from feeling a bit Light-hearted.

People will embody this energy in their souls, and it will make them feel lighter and happier and one step closer to awakening.

This feeling of hope and excitement is the first step towards awakening.

Prophecy 88

Received June 29, 2022

Happiness is a symptom of an open heart.

People who have closed hearts are much less happy.

People with open hearts tend to laugh more and see Light and Love in almost everything.

Before people can flow Love energy unrestricted, they must do their personal work, and as they complete their work, their heart opens more with each step.

Feeling hopeful and excited about the future is *the* sign that your heart is opening.

Give yourself credit for doing your personal work, and being open to hope and excitement about the future.

Just accomplishing that first step is a much bigger deal than anyone realizes.

Everyone on Earth deserves a huge pat on the back for a job done exceptionally well.

Prophecy 89

Received June 29, 2022

Life on Earth is the most challenging assignment any soul can sign up for.

Life born in a blank slate is a huge sacrifice to all others in the Universe.

The Universe will give Earth many gifts as an exchange for this sacrifice.

One of those gifts will be the ability to manifest a new reality in a new dimension while still living on Earth.

Lightworkers who flow Love energy unrestricted, will be rewarded with access to a new dimension on Earth.

This new dimension will allow these Lightworkers to create homes and lives in a space of Love and Light, within a community of other Lightworkers who flow Love energy unrestricted.

This other dimension will be an incredible space for Lightworkers to gather and spend time in Love energy.

This new dimension will exist on Universal time. That leaves all Earth time in suspension while Lightworkers are in this new dimension.

Lightworkers will be able to spend as much time as they wish in this new dimension, and not lose a single moment of Earth time.

Prophecy 90

Received June 29, 2022

Lightworkers are highly regarded across the Universe.

The other beings of the Universe are all in a flurry preparing to bring knowledge and gifts to the Lightworkers on Earth.

The other beings of the Universe are so excited and honoured with being able to help Lightworkers on Earth in any way possible.

The other beings in the Universe have watched Earth evolve, and understand the sacrifice Lightworkers have made by incarnating onto Earth over and over again.

The other beings of the Universe prepared for Earth's demise, instead of Earth's success. They are now in preparations for Earth's awakening.

The other dimension on Earth is now being constructed and filled with all kinds of treasures.

The other beings of the Universe are gathering ideas from the dreams of Lightworkers on Earth.

Lightworkers have dreams about what they wish to create in their lives, and the other beings of the Universe are putting these ideas into the other dimension they are creating for Earth.

When Lightworkers arrive in this dimension, they will be surprised that all their dreams are there, as well as some incredible things that humankind cannot even imagine.

Prophecy 91

Received June 29, 2022

This new dimension will be an incredible place, and some Lightworkers will choose to spend all of their time there.

Some Lightworkers will choose to visit Earth once in a while but spend most of their time in the other dimension.

These Lightworkers will not be the majority, however, they will exist, and they have a very important job to do in the other dimension of Earth.

These Lightworkers will have important creations to work on, and they will help to bring ancient knowledge back to Earth.

These Lightworkers will create new worlds on Earth that have special energies and special inhabitants.

These Lightworkers are going to re-create Atlantis and Lemuria and Perseun.

Prophecy 92

Received June 29, 2022

This new dimension on Earth is being created with the utmost care and Love.

Lightworkers will feel incredibly loved and appreciated when they arrive in this new dimension.

This is where new ideas and creations will come from.

This new dimension will be a creation space for Lightworkers to help others who have not yet awakened.

Lightworkers may create something in this new dimension, and it will be easier for people to then create that same thing on Earth.

Lightworkers will help others through this manifestation process. Once something is created in this new dimension, it becomes much easer for people on Earth to feel it and re-create it on Earth.

Prophecy 93

Received June 29, 2022

Some Lightworkers will choose to spend most of their time in this new dimension.

This does not mean that they will never return to Earth.

Most Lightworkers will visit the new dimension often, and return to Earth without missing a single moment.

The Lightworkers who will choose to spend their time in this new dimension will also return to Earth, but they will return for certain moments in time. They will be absent from Earth in between their visits.

These Lightworkers will focus their attention on creating things in the new dimension so that they will eventually be re-created on Earth.

These Lightworkers have a lot of work ahead of them.

Prophecy 94

Received June 29, 2022

Lightworkers will be amazed by the work that will occur in this new dimension.

This new dimension will bring incredible manifestations and technology to Earth.

This new dimension is a huge blessing for everyone on Earth.

Some Lightworkers will be able to manifest a lot of inventions, and once they appear on Earth, these Lightworkers will teach others how to use the inventions.

Some inventions will make life on Earth very pleasant, and others will make life on Earth very joyful, and others will give people a way to explore and enjoy all Earth has to offer.

These inventions will become more and more frequent as time goes on, and more and more Lightworkers have access to this new dimension.

One invention of special note will involve a new way to travel.

This new way to travel will not require a vehicle.

This new way to travel will involve creating a personal space-alteration that will allow a person to travel from one side of the world to another with very little effort.

This new way to travel will allow people to literally walk through an altered-space link to get from one area to another.

This new way to travel will come forth after the majority of people have awakened.

Prophecy 95

Received June 30, 2022

Very few people on Earth have a real sense of their own power.

Most people on Earth are working through karma that gives them a false sense of unworthiness and powerlessness.

The few people on Earth who are aware of their power are going to be surprised when others awaken to their own power. These people who are aware of their power have gained that power from others being powerless.

When people awaken to their own power, these people will lose theirs.

This is going to be a huge shock to them and it will be the beginning of the end of power imbalance on Earth.

These people who are aware of their own power will have a lot of personal work to do when that illusion falls away.

These people will need help from Lightworkers, and everyone can help by sending Love and Light energy to them to speed up their healing process.

The faster everyone does their work and heals their karma, the faster everyone gets to live their best lives on Earth.

Prophecy 96

Received June 30, 2022

Soon, Earth and its people will see many changes that many people thought would never occur.

The number of people that will begin to question everything is huge and somewhat overwhelming.

Lightworkers will become incredibly busy.

Lightworkers will become incredibly respected.

Once the Earth's energy begins to shift, the awakening process will speed up exponentially.

Lightworkers will be incredibly busy.

Lightworkers also need to remember to live their best lives, and that is ultimately the best way to help others awaken.

Everyone will awaken with or without help.

Lightworkers are going to love helping people awaken.

Lightworkers are going to love living their best lives.

Lightworkers need to balance these two important aspects of their lives.

Lightworkers need to give themselves as much time as they wish, to enjoy their own lives.

Prophecy 97

Received June 30, 2022

New and exciting adventures await the Lightworkers of Earth.

Some Lightworkers will eventually travel to other galaxies in the Universe.

These Lightworkers will bring back incredible knowledge to share.

These Lightworkers will create wonderful things on Earth with this knowledge.

Other galaxies in the Universe have been watching Earth since the beginning, and have been preparing for these visits and are extremely excited about having Lightworkers visit.

These visiting Lightworkers will be treated like royalty.

These visiting Lightworkers will be given special knowledge that will enable them to create things that are impossible to imagine now.

These Lightworkers will cherish their visits to other galaxies.

Prophecy 98

Received June 30, 2022

Some Lightworkers will become Masters of their special talents.

These Lightworkers will be able to teach other Lightworkers their special talents.

The Lightworkers who are Masters at a specific talent will also have a stronger Love energy in that specific talent.

Every Lightworker can learn any method, however, there are certain Lightworkers who have mastered a certain talent over many lifetimes, and they naturally carry more Love energy in that talent.

This Love energy makes their talent stronger than others.

This Love energy gives them the ability to share their talents with others through teaching. When a Lightworker teaches a talent to another Lightworker, they lend their Love energy to that Lightworker.

However, Love energy has a unique quality. Love energy multiplies when shared. So, as the Lightworker shares their Love energy with another Lightworker, they both receive a boost in Love energy.

Love energy is a wonderful thing.

Love is meant to be shared.

When Love is shared, many people benefit.

Love benefits the receiver, and Love benefits the giver, and Love benefits anyone who witnesses this exchange.

Love is beautiful.

Prophecy 99

Received June 30, 2022

This last prophecy is a big one.

Begin hoping that Love is about to be born.

Lightworkers on Earth have more power than they realize.

As a group of Light beings, Lightworkers carry a lot of collective power for change on Earth.

When Lightworkers carry a similar thought or hope or desire, they increase the energy behind it exponentially.

Lightworkers holding the same Hope are incredibly powerful for change.

So, begin hoping Love arrives on Earth.

ABOUT THE AUTHOR

Cindy is a proud and loving wife and mother who loves life. She laughs easily and tries to see the Light in everything. She strives to learn and grow every day. Cindy loves to travel both near and far, and encounter new adventures in surprising places. She experiences Joy in all kinds of things, big and small, and she loves ordinary days.